WATCH THEM
• • • • • • •
GROW!

The Life Cycle of a
KANGAROO

Amy Austen

PowerKiDS press™

New York

Published in 2016 by The Rosen Publishing Group, Inc.
29 East 21st Street, New York, NY 10010

First Edition

Editor: Caitie McAneney
Book Design: Reann Nye

Photo Credits: Cover Nagel Photography/Shutterstock.com; p. 5 Christopher Meder/Shutterstock.com; p. 6 mark higgins/Shutterstock.com; p. 9 Jami Tarris/Photographer's Choice/Getty Images; pp. 10, 23, 24 (kangaroo with joey) idiz/Shutterstock.com; pp. 13, 23 (joey) worldwildlifewonders/Shutterstock.com; pp. 15, 24 (kangaroo with joey in pouch) THPStock/Shutterstock.com; p. 16 Kjuuurs/Shutterstock.com; pp, 19, 23 (kangaroos) Ralph Loesche/Shutterstock.com; pp. 20, 23 (jumping kangaroo) picturepartners/Shutterstock.com.

Library of Congress Cataloging-in-Publication Data

Austen, Amy, author.
 The life cycle of a kangaroo / Amy Austen.
     pages cm. — (Watch them grow!)
 Includes index.
 ISBN 978-1-4994-0672-6 (pbk.)
 ISBN 978-1-4994-0674-0 (6 pack)
 ISBN 978-1-4994-0675-7 (library binding)
 1. Kangaroos—Life cycles—Juvenile literature. I. Title.
 QL737.M35A775 2016
 599.2'22—dc23
                          2014048538

Manufactured in the United States of America

CPSIA Compliance Information: Batch #WS15PK: For Further Information contact Rosen Publishing, New York, New York at 1-800-237-9932

Contents

A Kangaroo's Life   4

Tiny Joeys   8

Growing Tall!   18

Words to Know   24

Index   24

Websites   24

Have you ever seen a kangaroo? They can grow as tall as a person!

A kangaroo's body changes as it grows. The changes make up its life cycle.

7

Kangaroo mothers give birth to tiny babies. Baby kangaroos are called **joeys**.

pouch →

A joey is only about an inch (3 cm) long when it's born. It climbs into a **pouch** on its mother's belly.

A newborn joey is tiny and weak. It drinks milk inside its mother's pouch.

13

A joey lives in its mother's pouch for up to 10 months. The mother carries her joey everywhere!

A joey comes out of the pouch when it is big enough. It learns to hop!

A joey still drinks its mother's milk for a few months. It grows fast.

A joey grows into an adult kangaroo. It has big feet and a long tail.

A female adult kangaroo can give birth to her own joeys. A new life cycle starts!

Life Cycle of a Kangaroo

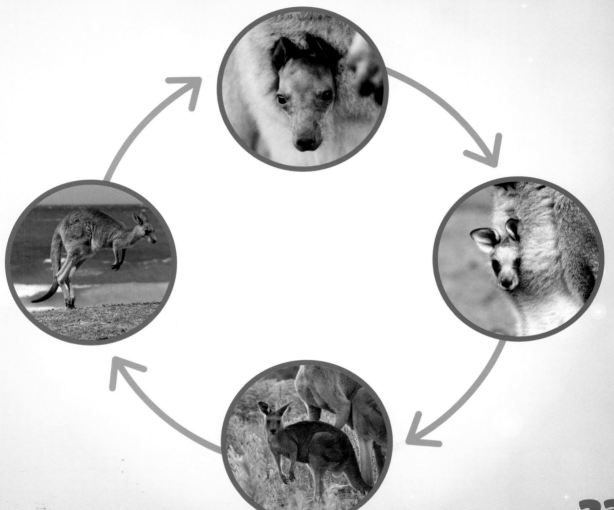

Words to Know

joey

pouch

Index

A
adult, 21, 22

J
joey, 8, 11, 12, 14, 17, 18,
    21, 22

M
mother, 8, 11, 12, 14, 18

P
pouch, 11, 12, 14, 17

Websites

Due to the changing nature of Internet links, PowerKids Press has developed an online list of websites related to the subject of this book. This site is updated regularly. Please use this link to access the list: www.powerkidslinks.com/wtg/kang